Preschool Art

Craft and Construction

MaryAnn F. Kohl
Illustrations: Katheryn Davis

Dedication

Dedicated in memory of my grandmother, Mary Geanne Faubion Wilson,
the first published author I ever knew, who sparked my imagination
when she told me that angels made my freckles
when they kissed me on the nose as I slept.

Acknowledgments

I would like to thank my editor, Kathy Charner, for her humor and kindness
in our editor-author relationship. Sometimes I think we have too much fun to call this work!
In addition, I would like to thank the owners of Gryphon House, Leah and Larry Rood,
for their support and friendship, and their belief in this book and in me.
Most important, my thanks go to my husband, Michael,
and my daughters, Hannah and Megan, who keep my mind clear,
tell me when I've been wonderful or when I haven't, and
remind me of what is most important in life.

Preschool Art

Craft and Construction

It's the process, not the product!

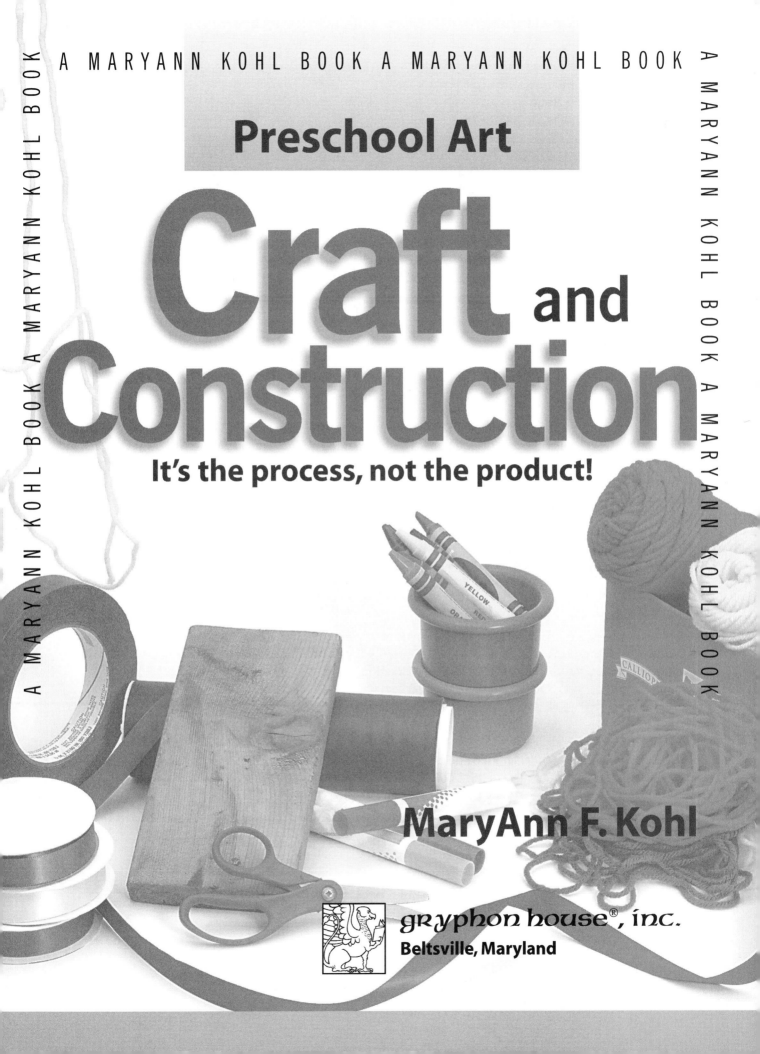

MaryAnn F. Kohl

gryphon house®, inc.

Beltsville, Maryland

Library of Congress Cataloging-in-Publication Data

Kohl, MaryAnn F.,
    Preschool art: it's the process, not the product! / MaryAnn F. Kohl; [illustrations, Katheryn Davis].
        p.   cm.
    "A MaryAnn Kohl book."
    Inludes indexes.
    Contents: [1] Craft and construction --[2] Clay, dough, and sculpture -- [3] collage and paper -- [4] Painting -- [5] Drawing.
    ISBN 0-87659-251-5 (v.1)
    1. Art--Study and teaching (Preschool)--Handbooks, manuals, etc. I. Title: craft and construction. II. Title: Clay, dough, and sculpture. III. Title: Collage and paper. IV. Title: Painting. V. Title: Drawing. VI. Davis, Katheryn. VII. Title.
LB1140.5.A7 K64 2001
372.5'044--dc21
                                                                           2001018468

Illustrations: Katheryn Davis
Cover photograph: Straight Shots Product Photography, Ellicott City, Maryland.

Bulk purchase

Gryphon House books are available at special discount when purchased in bulk for special premiums and sales promotions as well as for fund-raising use. Special editions or book excerpts also can be created to specification. For details, contact the Director of Marketing at the address above.

Disclaimer

The publisher and the author cannot be held responsible for injury, mishap, or damages incurred during the use of or because of the activities in this book. The author recommends appropriate and reasonable supervision at all times based on the age and capability of each child.

Table of Contents

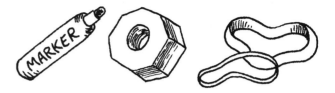

Introduction 6

Activities

It's the Process, Not the Product

Why is art process important?

Young children do art for the experience, the exploration, and the experimentation. In the "process" of doing art, they discover creativity, mystery, joy, and frustration, all important pieces in the puzzle of learning. Whatever the resulting masterpiece—be it a bright sticky glob or a gallery-worthy piece—it is only a result to the young child, not the reason for doing the art in the first place.

Art process allows children to explore, discover, and manipulate their worlds. Sometimes the process is sensory, such as feeling slippery cool paint on bare fingers. Other times it is the mystery of colors blending unexpectedly, or the surprise of seeing a realistic picture evolve from a random blob of paint. Art process can be a way to "get the wiggles out," or to smash a ball of clay instead of another child.

How can adults encourage the process of art?

Provide interesting materials. Stand back and watch. Offer help with unruly materials, but keep hands off children's work as much as possible. It's a good idea not to make samples for children to copy because this limits their possibilities.

Sometimes adults unknowingly communicate to a child that the product is the most important aspect of the child's art experience. The following comments and questions serve as examples of things to say that will help encourage each child to evaluate his or her own artwork:

Tell me about your artwork.	*How did the paint feel?*
What part did you like the best?	*The yellow is so bright next to the purple!*
I see you've used many colors!	*How did you make such a big design?*
Did you enjoy making this?	*I see you made your own brown color. How did you do it?*

Process art is a wonder to behold. Watch the children discover their unique capabilities and the joy of creating. This is where they begin to feel good about art and to believe that mistakes can be a stepping stone instead of a roadblock—in art as well as in other aspects of their lives. A concept children enjoy hearing is, "There's no right way, there's no wrong way, there's just your way."

Getting Ready!

Being prepared makes art experiences all the more enjoyable.
Here are some tips for success:

Covered Workspace

Cover the workspace—whether it is a table, floor, chair, wall, or countertop—with newspaper. Tape it down to prevent wiggles and spills of art materials. It's so much easier to bunch up sheets of paint-filled, sticky newspaper and find a clean space underneath than to clean up uncovered workspaces time and again. Other workspace coverings that work well are sheets of cardboard, an old shower curtain, a plastic table-cloth, big butcher paper, and roll ends of newsprint from the local newspaper print shop.

Handy Cleanup

Make cleanup easy and independent for young artists. All the less worry for the adult in charge! Place a wet sponge or pads of damp paper towels next to the art project for a simple way to wipe fingers as needed. Rather than have children running to the sink, fill a bucket with warm soapy water and place it next to the work area. Then add a few old towels for drying hands. Damp rags and sponges are handy for wiping spills, tidying up, and cleaning splatters as needed.

The Cover-up

Any old apron, Dad's old shirt (sleeves cut off), a smock, and a paint shirt are all helpful cover-ups for creative preschoolers. Instead, consider this: wear old play clothes and old shoes and call them "art clothes," used for art only. It's a wonderful feeling to get into art without being concerned about protecting clothing. These clothes become more unique with time and are often a source of pride!

Other Tips

- Create a separate drying area covered with newspapers. Allow wet projects to dry completely.
- Always protect a larger circle of space than the immediate area around the project. Think about floors, walls, and carpets (maybe even ceilings!).
- Shallow containers are often mentioned in the Materials lists. These include cookie sheets, flat baking pans, clean kitty litter trays, plastic cafeteria trays, painter's pans, and flat dishes and plates.
- It's never too late to start collecting recyclables for art. Save collage materials, fabric and paper scraps, Styrofoam grocery trays, yarn, sewing trims, and even junk mail.
- Wash hands thoroughly before starting any edible activity.
- Do activities inside or out unless specifically noted as an outdoor activity only.

Using the Icons

Each page has icons that help make the projects in Craft and Construction more useable and accessible. The icons are suggestions only. Experiment with the materials, vary the suggested techniques, and modify the projects to suit the needs and abilities of each child.

Age

The age icon indicates the general age range of when a child can create and explore independently without much adult assistance. The "& Up" means that older children will enjoy the project, and younger children might need more assistance. Children do not always fit the standard developmental expectations of a particular age, so decide which projects suit individual children and their abilities and needs.

Planning and Preparation

The plan and prep icon indicates the degree of planning or preparation time an adult will need to collect materials, set up the activity, and supervise the activity. Icons shown indicate planning that is easy or short, medium or moderate, or long and more involved.

Help

The help icon indicates the child may need extra assistance with certain steps during the activity from an adult or even from another child.

Caution

The caution icon appears for activities that use materials that may be sharp, hot, or electrical in nature. These activities require extra supervision and care.

Hints

Hints are suggestions for the adults working with the artists.

Lace and Sew

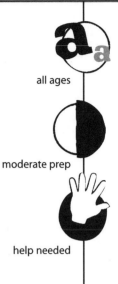

all ages

moderate prep

help needed

Materials

matte board,
   cardboard, or
   Styrofoam tray
scissors
colored yarn
hole punch
masking tape

Art Process 1—Lace and Wrap

1. Cut matte board or cardboard into square pieces.
2. Cut slits around the edges of a square of cardboard or matte board.
3. Cut colored yarn into 2′ (0.5 m) long pieces.
4. Pull the end of a piece of yarn through a slit in the cardboard and then wrap the yarn through another slit. Crisscross or wrap the cardboard square as desired.
5. Finish by tucking the end of the yarn through a slit and trimming it.

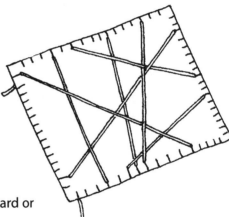

Art Process 2—"Needleless" Sewing

1. Punch holes around the edges of a square of cardboard or Styrofoam tray.
2. Tape the end of a piece of yarn with masking tape to make a needle-like end.
3. Push the taped end of the yarn through a hole, pull it through, and then push it through the next hole.
4. Continue "sewing" with the yarn until it runs out.
5. Tape the end down.
6. If desired, sew the square with more yarn.

Variations

- Using markers, color in the shapes between the yarn.
- Use embroidery thread instead of yarn.
- Use old greeting cards instead of cardboard.
- Use a large plastic darning needle. Thread the needle with a doubled 4′ (1.25 m) length of yarn, tie both ends in a knot, and begin sewing.

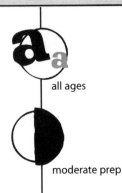
Junk and More Junk

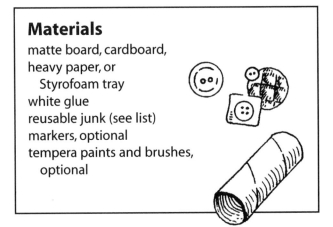

Materials

matte board, cardboard,
heavy paper, or
  Styrofoam tray
white glue
reusable junk (see list)
markers, optional
tempera paints and brushes,
  optional

Art Process

1. Place a piece of
   matte board,
   cardboard, heavy
   paper, or a Styrofoam
   tray on the work surface
   to form the base.
2. Glue "junk" (see list) together to make a three-dimensional project.
   Construct the object as desired—it can be tall, short, wide, or tiny. Build it so
   it rises from the base and has dimension.
3. Allow the project to dry completely.
4. Decorate the finished sculpture using pieces of fabric, markers, or paint.

Variations

- Use only one type of junk, such as a paper tube, an egg carton, rocks and
  sticks, or wood scraps to make constructions.
- Create a theme sculpture, such as Playground Trash, A Walk in the Woods,
  Broken Toys, or Happiness.

Junk Suggestions

bits of fabric and
  ribbon
buttons
cardboard boxes
corks
egg cartons
foil
paper tubes
pieces of toys
spools
wood scraps

Hints

- Save lots and lots of interesting "junk" and repeat over and over—artists will
  never have the same results twice!
- Use a glue gun for sturdy, quick gluing. Supervise closely.

Wood Creations

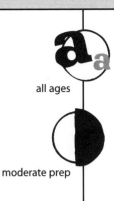

all ages

moderate prep

Materials

scraps of wood
matte board cardboard or square of wood,
    optional
white glue
decorating items (see list)

Art Process

1. Collect scraps of wood from a high school shop class or a picture frame shop. Ask members of wood shop classes to save curved, puzzle-like, and unusually shaped pieces.
2. If desired, use a piece of matte board or a square of wood as a base.
3. Glue pieces of scrap wood together, similar to building with blocks.
4. Allow the sculpture to dry overnight.
5. Decorate or paint the dry sculpture, if desired.

Variation

• Build a specific object, such as a house, bridge, or car.

Hints

• If a sculpture is top-heavy or unbalanced, white glue won't hold it well. Add some masking tape, rubber bands, or other supports until the glue has set. Remove the supports when the project is completely dry.
• For quicker results and stronger sculptures, use a glue gun. Supervise closely.

Decoration Suggestions

bits of collage
    materials
confetti
glitter
markers
nails
nuts and bolts
pieces of old toys
pieces of straws
ribbon
rubber bands
tempera paint

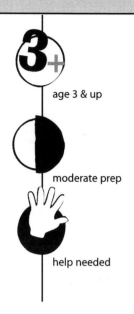

age 3 & up

moderate prep

help needed

Masterpiece Collection

Art Process

1. Choose a piece of artwork and glue or tape it into a blank scrapbook. Organize the book into specific sections or progress randomly throughout the year.
2. Write down comments or feelings about each piece of artwork placed in the scrapbook. (Do not write *on* the artwork.)
3. Continue to save artwork in the scrapbook until it is full.

<table>
<tr><td>

Materials
children's artwork
glue or tape
scrapbook with
   blank pages
markers

</td></tr>
</table>

Variations

• Create artwork directly on each scrapbook page.
• Make a homemade scrapbook. Stack large sheets of paper together. Punch holes into one side of the stack of paper and punch holes into a piece of cardboard to make a cover. String yarn through the holes to hold the scrapbook together. Save artwork or photographs in it.

Hint

• To help artists express their feelings about their artwork, ask them questions such as, "What did you like about this artwork?" or "Tell me about your masterpiece," or "Tell me about the colors you chose."

Tile Marking

Materials
white ceramic tiles
permanent, non-toxic markers

Art Process
1. Place white ceramic tiles on the work surface.
2. Draw on the tiles with permanent markers.
3. Tiles will dry quickly.

Variations
*   Use decorated tiles as trivets or hot pads to protect the table from hot dishes or foods. Glue cork or felt on the underside.
*   Decorated tiles make great gifts. Decorate the tiles with holiday themes for holiday gifts or decorations.

Hints
*   Ask building contractors for free leftover tiles, or contact a local home design store and ask for tile samples or leftovers.
*   Permanent markers can stain, so cover the table, the artist, or anything else in the work area that could be damaged.

Glue Over

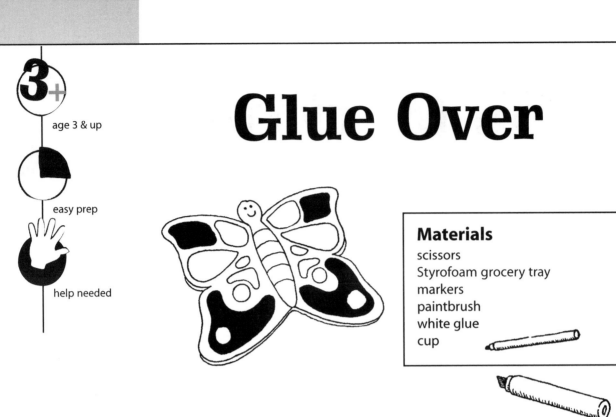

Materials

scissors
Styrofoam grocery tray
markers
paintbrush
white glue
cup

Art Process

1. Cut out a shape or piece from a Styrofoam grocery tray.
2. Draw on the piece of Styrofoam using a variety of colored markers. Completely cover the surface of the Styrofoam.
3. Allow the artwork to dry.
4. Pour white glue into a cup.
5. Paint glue over the entire surface of the colored Styrofoam piece.
6. Allow the glue to dry completely to produce a clear, slick, sealed surface that brightens and enhances the colors underneath.

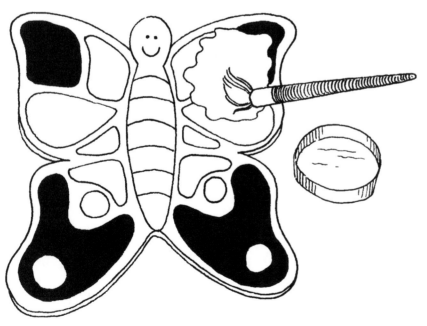

Variations

- Use the Glue Over as an ornament, hang it from a mobile, or hang it on a wall.
- To hang the Glue Over on the wall, poke a small hole in the Styrofoam and insert a bit of yarn. Or, tape a paper clip to the back of the design and use it as a hanger.

Hint

- Artists can make Glue Overs very small or very large depending on their choice, plan, or desire.

Tray Punch and Sew

age 3 & up

easy prep

help needed

caution

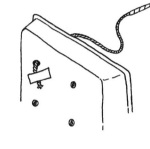

Materials
newspapers
Styrofoam grocery tray
scissors
pointed tool, such as a pencil or scissors point
colored yarn
masking tape

Art Process
1. Spread a thick pad of newspapers on the work table and put the Styrofoam grocery tray in the center, upside down.
2. Using a pointed tool such as a pencil, poke holes (not too many) into the tray. (If desired, choose a number such as 10, and poke only that many holes.)
3. Poke the holes in a random design or in a design that suggests a picture or shape. Add more holes at any time during the project, if desired.
4. Cut colored yarn into pieces about 2' (0.5 m) long.
5. Wrap a piece of masking tape around the end of a piece of yarn to resemble a needle.
6. Pull the yarn through a hole in the tray, but stop just before reaching the end.
7. Tape the end of the yarn to the back of the tray.
8. Continue sewing in and out of the holes to make a design. Change colors of yarn at any time.
9. When finished, tape the last end of yarn to the back of the tray.

Variations
- Thread the yarn on a large plastic needle and sew a design.
- Do not pre-poke holes in the Styrofoam tray. Instead, thread a plastic needle with yarn and poke holes as you sew, similar to embroidery.

Hint
- Young artists may need help threading a needle, taping the end of the yarn, and untangling the knots and loops that sometimes form.

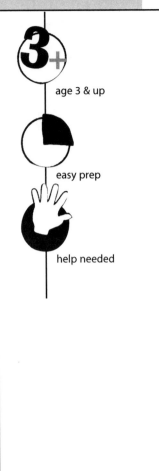

age 3 & up

easy prep

help needed

Bonnets

Materials

hole punch
paper plate
string or elastic
glue
decorative items
   (see list)
crayons, markers,
   or paints

Art Process

1. Punch a hole through opposite sides of a paper plate. Thread pieces of string or elastic through each hole. This will be the chinstrap to hold the finished bonnet in place.
2. Turn the plate upside down.
3. Glue decorations (see list) to the plate to create a bonnet. Use crayons, markers, or paint to decorate it.
4. For easier handling, decorate only the top of the bonnet and leave the underside undecorated. (If you want to decorate the underside, do so before decorating the top of the bonnet.)
5. Allow the bonnet to dry before wearing it.

Decorations

artificial flowers
beads
bows
confetti or glitter
fabric scraps
felt scraps
lace
ribbon
streamers

Variations

- Make a daintier design by using only tissue scraps, doilies, and foil.
- Create a "theme" bonnet, such as the environment, pets, or favorite colors.

Hint

- Attach one piece of elastic to both holes of the bonnet. Measure the elastic from one side of the bonnet, under the artist's chin, to the other side of the bonnet. No tying is necessary!

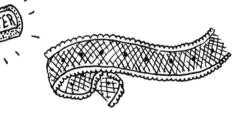

Parade

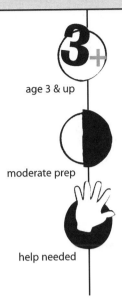

Materials

tricycles, bikes, big wheels, scooters, or wagons
decorating materials (see suggestions)
masking tape

Decorations

aluminum pie plates
balloons
crepe paper
flags
streamers
tin cans
yarn and string

Art Process

1. Decorate tricycles or other riding or pulling toys for a parade.
2. Decorating ideas include:
   - weaving crepe paper through bicycles spokes
   - tying balloons or streamers to handlebars
   - turning a wagon into a float
   - hanging noisy cans or pie plates on bikes
3. Start a parade around the playground, park, or down the neighborhood sidewalks.
4. Add marching people (decorate them too!), rhythm instruments, or noisemakers to the parade.

Variations

- Invite pets to join the parade.
- Play music on a tape recorder and march to the rhythm.

Hints

- Expect lots of enthusiasm and noise as part of the fun.
- Some children have no concept of staying in line or "following the leader" in a parade setting. To alleviate confusion, practice a bit before decorating. Straight lines are not necessarily important, but a parade does need some formation.

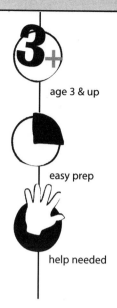

age 3 & up

easy prep

help needed

String Ornaments

Materials
string or
   embroidery floss
scissors
white glue
small bowl
water
wax paper
glitter

Art Process

1. Cut string or embroidery floss into pieces in a variety of lengths.
2. Pour glue into a small bowl and add water to thin it.
3. Dip a piece of string into the thinned glue.
4. Wipe off excess glue by pulling the string through the pointer finger and thumb or by pulling it across the edge of the bowl.
5. Place the string on a piece of wax paper in any shape, design, or pattern.
6. Sprinkle glitter over it.
7. Allow the string design to dry completely.
8. Gently peel the dry design from the wax paper.
9. Hang the string design as an ornament, if desired.

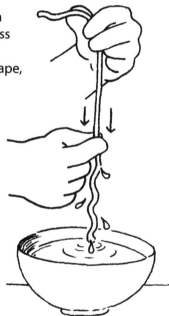

Variations

• Make specific shapes such as circles, stars, diamonds, or other designs.
• Create colored glue by adding tempera paint to the thinned glue.
• Sprinkle other materials onto the ornaments, such as colored sand or confetti.

Hints

• Allow this project to dry at least overnight.
• Peeling the string from the wax paper can be tricky.

Treasure Strings

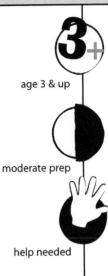

Materials

scissors
yarn
heavy, plastic needle
items to string
(see list)

Art Process

1. Cut a piece of yarn any length.
2. Thread a piece of yarn through a heavy, plastic needle.
3. Tie a knot into the far end of the yarn. Sometimes it helps to knot an item into the knot to form a barrier.
4. String any objects (see list) onto the yarn in a random or planned pattern.
5. Add more yarn, if desired, to make a very long necklace or a garland for decorating windows, walls, or doorways.
6. Make a necklace, bracelet, belt, or wall hanging.

Variation

- Plan a theme or use specific types of items for the project, such as beads from old jewelry; foil scraps, paper circles, and straw pieces; flower shapes and tissue sections; or toys and puzzle pieces.

Hints

- Young artists usually require help threading the yarn into the plastic needle and knotting the end of the yarn.
- If an artist has trouble pushing the plastic needle through some of the items, first poke holes using a hole punch, sharp pencil, or scissors point.

Items to String

buttons
egg carton cups
foil
hole-punched paper
  scraps
pieces of colored paper
sections of straws
sections of tissue rolls
spools
Styrofoam pieces

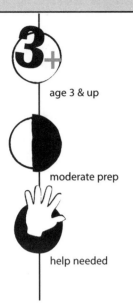

Boxes, Boxes

Art Process

1. Tape together boxes and tubes (see suggestions) to make abstract sculptures. Be creative—fit boxes inside one another, bend boxes to make new shapes, and cut boxes into new shapes.
2. String boxes together using heavy yarn.
3. Glue additional collage materials onto the boxes, as desired.
4. Pour tempera paint into bowls and add liquid dishwashing soap to it.
5. Paint the cardboard sculpture.
6. Allow the cardboard sculpture to dry overnight.

Variations

- Hang the box sculpture from the ceiling.
- Instead of creating an abstract sculpture, make animals, space-age cities, cars, rockets, dragon, boats, or other inventions or machines.

Hint

- Adding soap to the paint will help it stick to shiny or slick surfaces. It also makes washing paint out of clothing and off hands easier.

Materials

cardboard boxes
  (see suggestions)
masking tape
scissors
heavy yarn
white glue
collage materials,
  optional
thick tempera paint
bowls
liquid dish soap
paintbrushes

Box Suggestions

cardboard tube
jewelry box
liquor store box
milk carton
paper towel case box
plastic wrap box
shoebox
stationery box

Stuffed Stuff

Materials

markers or crayons
scraps of butcher paper
scissors
stapler
paint and brushes
glue, optional
collage materials, optional
newspaper or other scrap paper
yarn

STUFF WITH CRUMPLED PAPER!

Art Process

1. Draw a very large shape or design, such as a fish, pumpkin, animal, or abstract shape, on a 1-yard (1m) square sheet of butcher paper.
2. Cut out the shape from the butcher paper. To make two shapes at once, staple two sheets of butcher paper together and cut them at the same time.
3. Decorate both sides of the shape using markers, crayons, or paint. Glue additional materials to the design, if desired.
4. Secure the two shapes together by stapling the outside edges. Leave an opening on one side of the shape.
5. Stuff the shape with bunched-up newspaper or other paper scraps, filling out the shape.
6. Staple the opening.
7. If desired, add yarn and hang the Stuffed Stuff from the ceiling.

Variations

- Stuff the shape with a gift, prizes, candy, rewards, or other fun items. Give it to someone special.
- Make an entire zoo, undersea world, or crazy-shape garden out of Stuffed Stuff.

age 3 & up

involved prep

help needed

caution

Impress Wall Pot

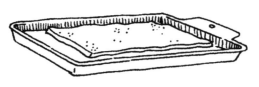

Art Process

1. Place two balls of Baker's clay on the table and roll each one flat.
2. Put one of the flat pieces on a cookie sheet as the base.
3. Make impressions in the other piece of clay by pressing toys, buttons, or other items into it.
4. Using a spatula, carefully lift the decorated piece of clay and place it on top of the plain piece on the cookie sheet.
5. Lift the top edge of the top piece of clay to create an envelope-like opening. Press the rest of the edges together, using a fork or pinching it closed with your fingers.
6. Poke two small holes in the top of the clay envelope (to hang it later).
7. Turn on the oven to 300° F and place the cookie sheet into it. Bake the clay pot for about 1 to 2 hours, or until it is nicely browned and hard.
8. Remove the pot from the oven and allow it to cool.
9. When the pot is cool, stick bits of weeds, dried flowers, or grasses into the opening of the "envelope."
10. Insert a piece of yarn through the holes in the design and hang the finished pot on the wall.

Hint

- Experiment and explore with various dough and clays before attempting to make this project.

Materials

Baker's clay (see recipe to the left)
rolling pin
cookie sheet
toys, buttons, nuts, bolts, pencils, or other items
spatula
fork
oven
oven mitts
dried weeds and grasses
yarn

Baker's Clay

bowl
flour
measuring cups
salt
water

Mix 1 cup (250 g) salt, 4 cups (500 g) flour, and 1 ½ cups (360 ml) water in a bowl. Knead the mixture for 5 minutes until it is soft and pliable.

PRESS ITEMS
INTO CLAY
TO MAKE DESIGNS

Colorful Stir Sticks

Materials
warm water
baking pan
powdered dye or food
  coloring
wooden coffee stir sticks
tongs or wide spatula
newspaper
masking tape

Art Process
1. Pour warm water into a baking pan.
2. Mix powdered dye or food coloring into the warm water. Make several pans of different colors, if desired.
3. Place wooden stir sticks into the warm dye.
4. Remove the sticks with tongs or a spatula. Place them on a piece of newspaper to dry.
5. Allow the wooden sticks to dry for several hours or overnight.
6. Build structures with the dry stir sticks by taping them together with bits of masking tape.

Variation
- To make a holiday or Valentine theme, glue little paper hearts or lace to the finished structure.

Hint
- Warm dye colors the wood faster than cool dye.
- The dye also colors hands and fingers, so wear rubber gloves or use tongs to remove the wet sticks from the dye.
- Dye matchsticks, craft sticks, or other wooden items.

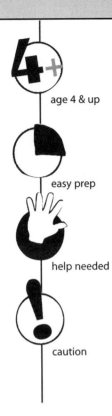

age 4 & up

easy prep

help needed

caution

Light Holes

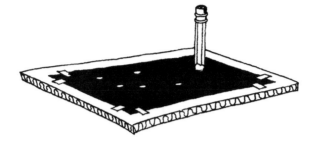

Art Process

1. Tape a sheet of black paper to a cardboard work surface.
2. Punch holes in the black paper using a poking tool. Make as many holes in as many sizes as desired.
3. Remove the tape.
4. Cover the holes with colored paper. Glue or tape the colored paper to the back of the black paper. Or, cover each hole with a small scrap of cellophane to create a special effect.
5. Place the Light Holes design in a window or hold it up to the light to see the colored lights.

Variations

- Cut the black paper into a pattern, such as a tree, star, or circle.
- Poke holes into a piece of colored paper and tape it to a sheet of black paper—the holes will appear to "pop out."
- Glue the Light Holes paper to a sheet of foil to create shiny holes.
- Put a piece of plywood on the work surface and use a hammer and nails to make the holes.

Hints

- Supervise this project closely. Allow plenty of room between artists and set a rule that artists must leave all sharp objects on the table.
- Some artists have not mastered how to poke holes through paper. They may tear the paper rather than make a hole. If the paper tears, tape the back of it or incorporate the tear into the final design.

Foil Treasures

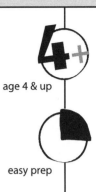

age 4 & up

easy prep

Materials

white glue
small three-dimensional
 items (see list)
cardboard
old paintbrush
heavy-duty aluminum foil
tape

Art Process

1. Glue a selection of small, three-dimensional objects onto a piece of cardboard.
2. Use an old paintbrush to paint white glue over the surface of the cardboard and all of the objects.
3. Carefully place a large sheet of aluminum foil over the raised surfaces of the glued objects.
4. Gently mold and press the foil around the objects to reveal their shapes. Be careful not to tear the foil.
5. Fold excess foil around the back of the cardboard. Tape or glue it into place.

Variation

- To create an antique effect, paint the aluminum foil with black paint. Before the paint dries, wipe it off, leaving some paint in the creases and wrinkles.

Hints

- Expect the objects to tear through the foil during first attempts with this project.
- Wash the paintbrush thoroughly before the glue dries on it.

Small three-dimensional Items

beads
bolts
buttons
golf tees
nuts
paper clips
pieces of yarn
rubber bands
washers

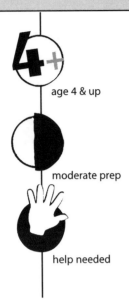

age 4 & up

moderate prep

help needed

Stick Wrapping

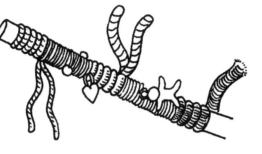

Materials

materials to wrap
  (see list)
3' (1 m) long stick
  or ½" – ¾"
  (1.5 cm –2 cm)
  dowel
masking tape
glue
decorations, such
  as feathers, felt,
  foil, or flowers
  with stems

Art Process

1. Select a material, such as yarn, to wrap around a 3' (1m) long stick. Tie a half-hitch knot or use masking tape to securely attach the yarn to the stick.
2. Wrap the yarn tightly around the stick.
3. Change colors or materials at any time. Tie the new material to the previous piece of yarn or tape it to the stick. Leave loose ends hanging or neatly tuck them in.
4. Tie, tape, glue, or wrap other decorative items into the yarn or string.
5. If desired, decorate loose ends with interesting items.

Variation

• Make a large rendition of a wrapped stick. Wrap a pillar or column with larger strips of fabric, colored rope, and yarn.

Hints

• Some young artists may find it difficult to wrap tightly. Use tape to help attach the yarn to the stick.
• Shorter sticks work well for younger artists. Working in pairs can also be helpful; one artist can wrap the stick while the second artist holds it.

Materials to Wrap

embroidery floss
fabric strips
ribbon
streamers
string
yarn

TAPE

HALF-HITCH
KNOT

①

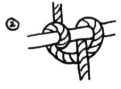
②

③

Boats

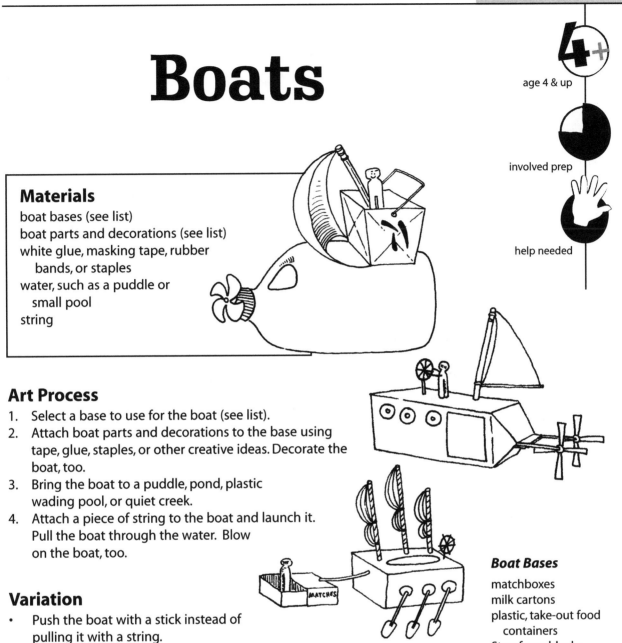

Materials

boat bases (see list)
boat parts and decorations (see list)
white glue, masking tape, rubber
    bands, or staples
water, such as a puddle or
    small pool
string

Art Process

1. Select a base to use for the boat (see list).
2. Attach boat parts and decorations to the base using tape, glue, staples, or other creative ideas. Decorate the boat, too.
3. Bring the boat to a puddle, pond, plastic wading pool, or quiet creek.
4. Attach a piece of string to the boat and launch it. Pull the boat through the water. Blow on the boat, too.

Variation

• Push the boat with a stick instead of pulling it with a string.

Hints

• Some boats will not float very well. Therefore, young artists may wish to test their boats in the sink first, make adjustments, and then launch their boats.
• Masking tape holds very well even when wet; cellophane tape does not.

Boat Bases

matchboxes
milk cartons
plastic, take-out food
    containers
Styrofoam blocks

Boat Parts and Decorations

clear contact paper
cotton balls
craft sticks
drinking straws
foil
kebab skewers
paper
plastic bags
stick-on paper
    reinforcements
toothpicks

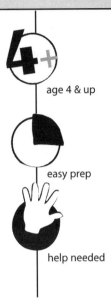

age 4 & up

easy prep

help needed

Circle Weave

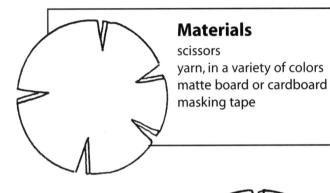

Materials

scissors
yarn, in a variety of colors
matte board or cardboard
masking tape

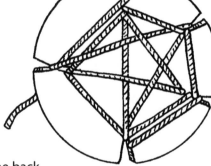

Art Process

1. Cut yarn into pieces 2' (0.5 m) long.
2. Cut cardboard or matte board into circles of any size.
3. Cut about five or six slits around the edges of each circle.
4. Wind the yarn around and around the circle shape, weaving it through the slits. Experiment making criss-cross designs.
5. Tape or tie the end of the yarn onto the back of the circle. Bend in the edges between the slits, if desired.

Variations

- Cut other shapes from the matte board or cardboard, such as a tree, square, or heart.
- Use embroidery floss or dental floss instead of yarn.

Hints

- A manageable size circle for young artists is about 5" (12 cm) across.
- To make an easy yarn dispenser, place a ball of yarn in a margarine cup. Cut a hole in the lid of the cup and pull the yarn through it. Snap on the lid and unwind the yarn without tangling it.

Neon Weave

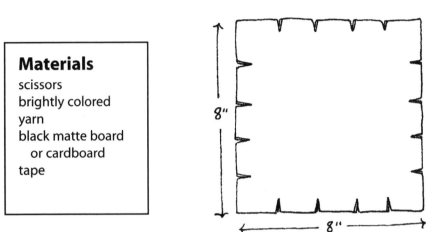

Materials

scissors
brightly colored
yarn
black matte board
  or cardboard
tape

Art Process

1. Cut bright yarn in a variety of different lengths, none exceeding 6′ (2 m).
2. Cut the black matte board or cardboard into 8″ x 8″ (20 cm x 20 cm) squares.
3. Cut slits about ½″ (1 cm) deep and 1″ – 2″ (2.5 cm – 5 cm) apart around each side of the square. (If desired, space slits farther apart from each other).
4. Tape the end of a piece of yarn to the back of the square and pull it through one of the slits.
5. Cross the yarn back and forth over the front of the square, pulling it through the slits. Pull it through the same slits as often as desired.
6. When one color of yarn runs out, tape another color of yarn to the back of the square. Continue to wrap, weave, cross, and decorate the square.
7. When finished, tape the end of the last piece of yarn to the back of the square or simply pull it through one of the slits.

Hint

• For easy yarn distribution, roll the yarn into a ball and place it in a cardboard box with a lid. Punch a hole in the lid, feed the yarn through the hole, and place the lid back on the box. Cut a slit in the edge of the lid to tuck the loose end of the yarn until the next person uses it. Make many holes and place many balls of yarn in the box.

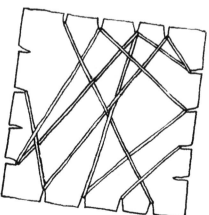

age 4 & up

moderate prep

help needed

caution

Basket Stitching

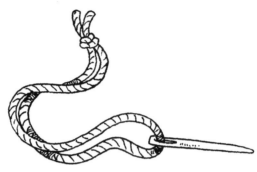

Art Process

1. Cut yarn into pieces varying in length.
2. Thread a fairly long piece of yarn through a plastic darning needle.
3. Begin stitching the yarn through the holes in a small cane basket. Stich in a random or planned design.
4. Change colors of yarn as desired.

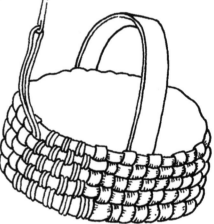

Hints

- When threading the needle, young artists may want to use double yarn that is tied at one end.
- Provide plenty of space between artists so no one gets poked with a needle.
- The firmness of the basket makes it easy for young artists to hold and push the needle through it.
- Inexpensive baskets used to hold paper plates also work well for this project.

Metal Cloth Stitchery

age 4 & up

moderate prep

help needed

Materials

scissors
metal cloth, sometimes called hardware cloth
masking tape
blunt, plastic yarn needle
yarn, string, or embroidery floss

Art Process

1. Cut a piece of metal cloth into 6" x 6" (15 cm x 15 cm) squares.
2. Cover the rough edges of the metal cloth with masking tape.
3. Thread a plastic needle with yarn, string, or embroidery floss.
4. Push the needle in and out of the holes of the metal cloth, creating patterns or designs.
5. Add other colors of yarn.
6. When finished, tie or tape the yarn to the back of the hardware cloth.

Variation

*   Stitch other material into the design, such as old beads, feathers, ribbons, pieces of lace, bits of paper, or confetti.

Hints

*   Metal cloth is a screen with 1/4" (6 mm) holes and is available at hardware stores. It is often used for the tops of hamster cages. An alternative to metal cloth is soffet screen, which is a more pliable screen on a roll.
*   Young artists may have difficulty stitching if the yarn is too long. A good length to use is an arm's length of yarn.

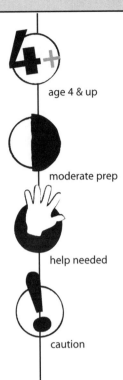

Weaving Board

Art Process

1. Put on a pair of safety glasses.
2. Hammer nails about ¼" to 1" (0.5 cm to 2.5 cm) apart along two edges of a flat board (supervise closely). Hammer in the nails tight and firm, but make sure they do not poke through the wood.
3. Wrap heavy string back and forth from one end of the board to the other. Begin with the first nail and end with the last nail.
4. Securely tie the string. This heavy string is called the warp string.
5. Push colorful yarn, ribbon, strips of fabric, or other long material (called the woof string) under and over the heavy wrap strings.
6. Change colors and materials, if desired, and continue weaving in any form or pattern, weaving one loose end to the beginning of the next.
7. Weave until the warp strings are completely full with color and design.
8. Remove the weaving from the nails or leave the artwork on the weaving board and display it.

Materials

safety glasses
hammer
finishing nails, no head
flat scrap of wood
heavy string
yarn, fabric strips, ribbon, dry grass, sewing trim, crepe paper, or raffia
scissors

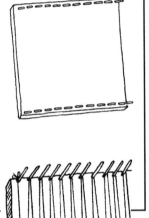

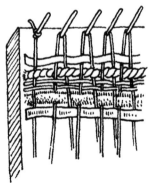

Hint

- Encourage the artists to explore using many weaving materials and activities. Then, demonstrate the over-under technique and other patterns, such as over-two-under-one.

Walking Puppets

Materials

scissors
artist's drawing
white glue
stiff paper or cardboard

↑ CUT OUT TWO HOLES ¼" APART

Art Process

1. Cut out a drawing and glue it to a piece of stiff paper or cardboard.
2. Cut two holes about ¼" (6 mm) apart at the base of the drawing. Cut each hole large enough to allow a finger poke through.
3. Put two fingers through the holes in the puppet. Your fingers will become the legs of the puppet.

Variations

• Put one puppet on each hand and put on a show or tell a story.
• Combine puppets with several artists and present a show with several characters.

Hints

• Use old file folders for stiff paper.
• Any drawing can be a puppet. The puppet does not have to be an animal or a person; even a design can be puppet.

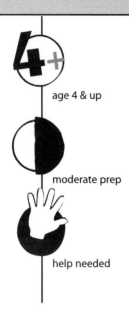

age 4 & up

moderate prep

help needed

Cuff Finger Puppets

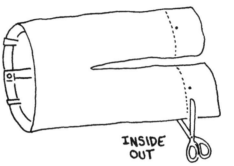

INSIDE OUT

Materials

old pair of pants
with deep cuffs
or hem
scissors
sewing machine
decorations (see
list)
tacky glue or
needle and
thread

Art Process

1. Take an old pair of pants with deep cuffs and turn them inside out.
2. Cut the pants straight across the hem.
3. Sew two "U" shapes into each cuff, so that the hem of the cuff will form the bottom of each finger puppet.
4. Cut ⅓" (8 mm) from the edge of the sewn line. Turn the cuff right side out or leave as is.
5. Decorate the cuff puppets by gluing or sewing a variety of sewing or craft items onto them. Create animals, people, characters from a book or story, or strange little shapes.
6. Make up plays or songs, or simply enjoy the puppets.

Decorations

sewing scraps
yarn
buttons
plastic eyes
felt

Variation

- Decorate a box to store a growing collection of cuff puppets. Create a group of puppets, such as three cuff bears and one golden-haired cuff girl and store them together.

Hint

- Artists can make approximately four cuff puppets from each pair of pants.

AFTER CUFF IS CUT, NOTE DOT

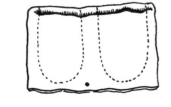

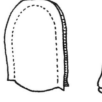

AFTER TURNING...

Easy Store Puppet Stage

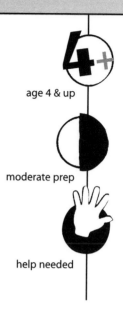

age 4 & up

moderate prep

help needed

Materials

spring-tension curtain
  rod that fits a
  doorway
tacky glue
tempera paint
spoon
small dishes
old sheet
fabric pens
paintbrushes
sewing machine,
  optional

Art Process

1. Place a spring-tension curtain rod in a doorway at a suitable height.
2. Make glue paint by mixing tacky glue and tempera paint. Place each color into a separate dish.
3. Decorate an old sheet using fabric pens or glue paint to create a puppet curtain.
4. Allow the puppet curtain to dry.
5. Drape the sheet over the curtain rod.
6. Or, sew a simple casing at the top of the sheet. Push the curtain rod through the casing and place it in the doorway.
7. Crouch behind the curtain and present a puppet show.
8. To store the puppet stage, roll the curtain around the rod and put it in a corner or closet.

Variation

- Add glitter to wet glue paint to make a glamorous curtain.

Hint

- Sometimes puppeteers need help ending a long production. Gently hint that the show will end in a few more minutes.

age 4 & up

involved prep

help needed

caution

Big Spooky House

Art Process

1. Cut a cardboard panel to look like a house. Cut a roof shape at the top and add as many doors and windows as desired. Leave one side of the door and window openings "hinged," so they will open and shut. Or, cut a "capital I" shape into the windows and doors, open them from the center, and fold them back.
2. Place the panel flat on the floor and paint boards, bricks, shutters, shingles, and other details onto the house.
3. Allow the house to dry completely.
4. Draw spooky pictures on paper large enough to fit over the window and door openings. Draw ghosts, bats, pumpkins, trick-or-treaters, and other spooky images.
5. Tape the pictures behind the window and door openings so the tape doesn't show.
6. Lean the spooky house panel against a wall or door. Secure it with tape or another method so that it stands on its own.
7. Enjoy opening and closing the doors and windows to reveal the spooky designs.

Materials

large cardboard panel
knife and scissors
tempera paint
paintbrushes
crayons
paper
masking tape

Variation

- Instead of making a spooky Halloween theme, design a house, tree, or vehicle with other types of characters inside. Some suggestions include forest creatures, storybook characters, or aliens from another planet.

Hints

- Prepare yourself for screams of delight!
- Make smaller spooky houses using construction paper or smaller pieces of cardboard.

Napkin Rings

4+

age 4 & up

easy prep

help needed

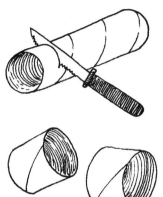

Materials
knife or scissors
cardboard tube
tempera paints
brushes
art tissue paper
liquid starch
clear contact paper

Art Process
1. Cut a cardboard tube, such as an empty paper towel holder, into 2" (5 cm) sections.
2. Paint the sections or rings using a single color of tempera paint.
3. Allow the rings to dry. Apply a second coat of paint.
4. When the second coat is dry, paint designs onto the rings. Or, attach pieces of art tissue using liquid starch.
5. Allow the rings to dry.
6. Cover each ring with a strip of clear contact paper to protect napkins from paint or tissue stains.

Variations
- Decorate the rings using markers instead of paint.
- Cover the rings with papier-mâché. Paint the rings when dry.
- Instead of using contact paper, coat the rings with clear, gloss enamel for a hard, clear finish.

Hint
- Place rings on a dowel or bottle top to dry.

Bottle Bank

Art Process

1. Pour glue into a small dish. Add water to make it a thin consistency.
2. Remove the lid of a glass jar or bottle and stand it upside down.
3. Tear colored tissue into small pieces.
4. Paint a small amount of thinned glue on one area of the jar.
5. Press a piece of tissue onto the glued area, and then paint more glue over it.
6. Continue adding more tissue pieces to the bottle the same way. Paint glue over the edges of the tissue and overlap pieces.
7. Glue the pieces of tissue as close to the opening of the bottle as possible without extending it over the edge or inside the bottle. (Test to make sure the lid of the jar still fits.)
8. Allow the project to dry.
9. Put the lid on a block of wood, right side up.
10. Put on a pair of safety glasses.
11. Place a screwdriver or a chisel point against the lid. Hit the handle with a hammer and drive the tool through the lid to make an opening for coins. If necessary, hammer several more cuts to make an opening for quarters. (Supervise this step very closely. Adults may want to do this step for the artists.) Turn the lid over and pound the sharp edges down with the hammer, if necessary.
12. Screw the lid onto the dry bottle and begin saving money.

Hints

- Smooth out any wrinkles in the tissue using the paintbrush.
- One layer of tissue should be enough for this project. However, young artists often like to pile on several layers of tissue paper, so be prepared.

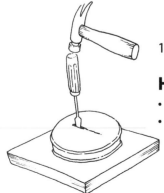

Life-Size Animal

Materials

large- and medium-size
cardboard boxes
wide masking tape or duct
tape
wheat paste
large tub or bucket
newspaper
small, damp towel, optional
fabric scraps, sewing scraps,
or colored paper
tempera paints and paint-
brushes

Art Process

1. Assemble a cardboard animal using medium- and large-size boxes. Rearrange the boxes as often as needed before taping them together.
2. When satisfied with the size and configuration, tape the box animal together.
3. Pour wheat paste into a large tub or bucket.
4. Tear newspaper into half sheets. Place a half sheet of newspaper in the wheat paste and briefly soak it until it is wet and coated.
5. Squeeze out the excess paste. Press the sheet of newspaper over the animal shape. Press out the wrinkles using your bare hands or a damp, small towel.
6. Completely cover the box animal with layers of newspaper. Add extra bumps, curves, and features with balls, lumps, or mounds of soaked paper, if desired.
7. Allow the sculpture to dry for several days, until it is crunchy and hollow sounding.
8. Paint the box animal or decorate it with fabrics and papers.

Hint

- Artists love to build really large objects. Working with wheat paste and newspaper is messy, but this is compensated by the artists' creativity and joy of sculpting something life-sized.

Craft & Construction   **39**

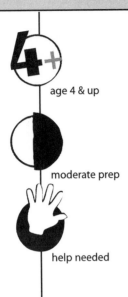

age 4 & up

moderate prep

help needed

Stuffed Fabric

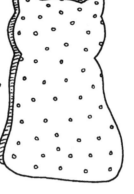

PLACE TWO LAYERS
TOGETHER, RIGHT SIDES
OUT...

Materials

scissors
plain or patterned
   fabric squares
pencil or crayon
fabric pens,
   optional
fabric glue, in a
   bottle
pillow stuffing or
   fabric scraps
stapler
pinking shears

Art Process

1. Cut the fabric into 8" (20 cm) squares.
2. Draw a design or shape on a square of fabric. Re-draw the exact design on another square of fabric.
3. Cut out the shapes from the fabric.
4. Decorate the fabric using fabric pens, if desired.
5. Place the two identical shapes together, undecorated sides of the fabric touching (right sides out).
6. Glue the edges of the fabric together, leaving one side open for stuffing.
7. Allow the project to dry overnight.
8. Stuff the shape with fabric scraps or pillow stuffing.
9. Glue the open edge of the shape together. If it doesn't hold, staple it and remove the staples after the glue dries.
10. Trim the edges with pinking shears or scalloping scissors.

Variations

- Make stuffed toys, tree decorations, or little dolls for big dolls to play with.
- Sew the shape using a sewing machine or a needle and thread.

Hint

- Use fabric glue that is labeled "Fast Drying" or "Good for Seams."

Paper Strip Construction

Materials

scissors
construction paper
Styrofoam grocery
    tray
tape, glue, or
    stapler
paper punch

Art Process

1. Cut construction paper into strips.
2. Attach one end of a construction paper strip to the Styrofoam base using a stapler, glue, or tape.
3. Secure another strip to the first strip using tape, glue, or a stapler.
4. Continue adding strips of paper to the base or to other paper strips to create a three-dimensional paper construction. Pleat, fold, cut, hole-punch, or connect the strips. Let imaginations soar!
5. Allow the project to dry (if it was glued).

Variations

*   Add other items to the construction, such as paper shapes, glitter, confetti, or magazine pictures. Sew and tie pieces of yarn to the sculpture, too.
*   Use matte board or wood for the base.
*   Create a sculpture using other types of paper, such as computer paper or wrapping paper. Join the paper together using stickers or paper clips.

Hint

*   Paper Strip Construction is interesting because of the intersection of paper strips; it does not need to "be" anything or look like anything.

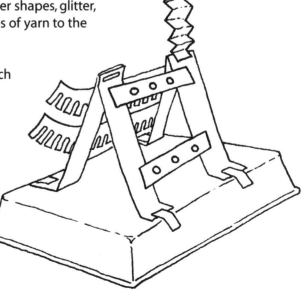

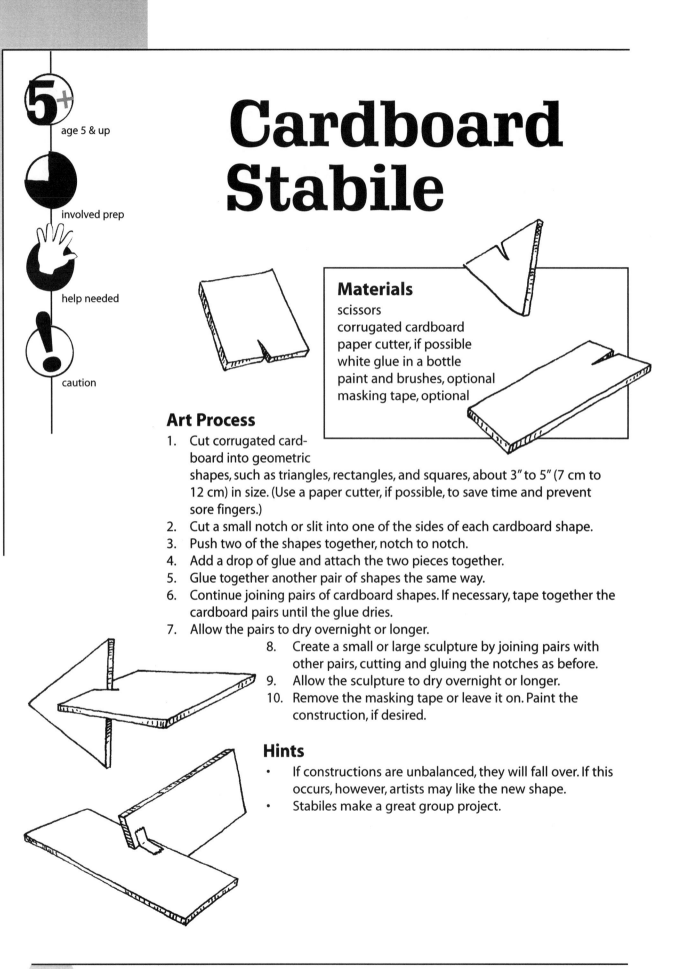

Cardboard Stabile

Materials
scissors
corrugated cardboard
paper cutter, if possible
white glue in a bottle
paint and brushes, optional
masking tape, optional

Art Process
1. Cut corrugated cardboard into geometric shapes, such as triangles, rectangles, and squares, about 3" to 5" (7 cm to 12 cm) in size. (Use a paper cutter, if possible, to save time and prevent sore fingers.)
2. Cut a small notch or slit into one of the sides of each cardboard shape.
3. Push two of the shapes together, notch to notch.
4. Add a drop of glue and attach the two pieces together.
5. Glue together another pair of shapes the same way.
6. Continue joining pairs of cardboard shapes. If necessary, tape together the cardboard pairs until the glue dries.
7. Allow the pairs to dry overnight or longer.
8. Create a small or large sculpture by joining pairs with other pairs, cutting and gluing the notches as before.
9. Allow the sculpture to dry overnight or longer.
10. Remove the masking tape or leave it on. Paint the construction, if desired.

Hints
- If constructions are unbalanced, they will fall over. If this occurs, however, artists may like the new shape.
- Stabiles make a great group project.

Harvest Art

5+

age 5 & up

moderate prep

help needed

Materials

leftover harvest foods or outside items (see list)
toothpicks, bamboo skewers, or string
bits of paper, play clay, feathers, or dried flowers
non-toxic permanent
markers

MARKER

Art Process

1. Go for a walk in a field, orchard, or garden and collect leftover harvest foods or other outdoor materials.
2. Assemble the Harvest Art using string, skewers, toothpicks, or other materials. Create cornhusk royalty, corn folks, nut puppets, stick marionettes, feather birds, leaf masks, or any other imaginative mobiles or designs.
3. Add berries to make eyes or bits of paper to make capes and hats. Use markers to make detailed features.
4. Bring the art home and enjoy it or leave it outside for critters to discover and eat.

Variation

• Build little houses for the harvest creatures using ferns, moss, sticks, and holes dug into the earth. Add roads, worlds, and more worlds.

Hints

• There is no right or wrong way to create Harvest Art. The fun is being outside on a crisp day, hunting for treasures from the earth.
• Most Harvest Art creations do not hold together well enough for robust play. Artists will enjoy creating the art and playing with it the day they make it, but prepare to discard it soon after.

Harvest Foods

berries
cornhusks
leaves
nuts
twigs

Branch Weaving

Materials

scissors
yarn, in many colors
   and textures
tree branch with at
   least 3 smaller
   branches
   shooting out
materials to weave
   (see list)

Materials to Weave

cords
cornhusks
feathers
long grasses
ribbons
strings
strips of fabric
weeds
wool

Art Process

1. Cut the yarn into pieces
    about 2' (0.5 m) long.
2. Starting at the top or bottom
    of one of the small branches, loop a piece of yarn
    around it.
3. Wrap yarn around the smaller branches,
    making a base of yarn that moves up or
    down the branches.
4. Weave yarn, wool, grasses, fabric strips, or
    any other intriguing items into the yarn
    base. Randomly weave and wrap as
    desired.

Variation

*   Nail or glue strips of thin wood to a
    wood frame or box shape. Wrap and
    weave yarn around the wood base.

Hint

*   If the pieces of yarn are longer than 2' (0.5 m), they tend to get tangled. If
    the pieces are too short, they run out too quickly. Simply add more yarn as
    each piece runs out.

King-Size Rope Wrap

age 5 & up

moderate prep

help needed

caution

Materials

safety glasses
hammer
nails with large heads, less than ½″ (1.5 cm) long
square of plywood, at least ½″ (1.5 cm) thick and 2′ (70 cm) square
rope, yarn, string, or cord
feathers, cotton balls, ribbon, or other decorative odds and ends, optional

Art Process

1. Put on a pair of safety glasses.
2. Hammer nails into a square of plywood in any design. Hammer nails around the edges or in the center of the square (supervise closely). Be careful not to hammer the nails all the way through the plywood and into the floor or table.
3. Wind, wrap, tie, and weave rope or yarn around the various nails to form colorful designs.

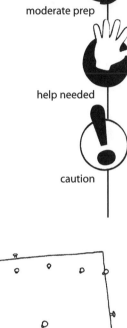

4. Add optional decorations, such as feathers or cotton balls, to the yarn or rope as desired.

Variations

- Make this a group project by using a larger sheet of plywood and more nails.
- Before hammering nails into the wood, paint it or cover it with wrapping paper or contact paper.

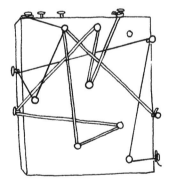

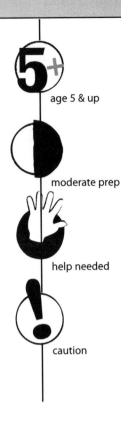

age 5 & up

moderate prep

help needed

caution

Paper Bag Kite

Art Process

1. Punch a hole into each of the four corners of a paper bag, about ½" (1 cm) from the edge.
2. Stick a reinforcement circle over each hole.
3. Cut two pieces of string about 1 yard (1 m) long.
4. Tie each end of one of the strings into a reinforced hole to form a loop. Make a loop with the second string, too.
5. Cut another piece of string about 1 yard (1 m) long. Pull it through the two loops and tie it. (This will form the kite handle.)
6. Paint the bag as desired.
7. Allow the paint to dry.
8. Glue kite decorating materials (see list) to the paper bag kite.
9. Allow the kite to dry completely.
10. Take the kite outside. Open the bag, hold onto the string, and run. The wind will catch in the bag and the kite will fly out and above you.

Materials

hole punch
large paper grocery bag
stick-on paper
    reinforcements
scissors
string
paints and brushes
white glue
kite decorating materials
    (see list)

Kite Decorating Materials

crepe paper
paper liners for muffin
    tins or candy cups
paper scraps and
    collage materials
ribbons
streamers
tissue paper

Hints

- For the strongest and most successful kite experience, allow the bag to dry completely between painting, decorating, and flying it.
- To make the kite last longer, add extra reinforcements or clear contact paper to the holes.

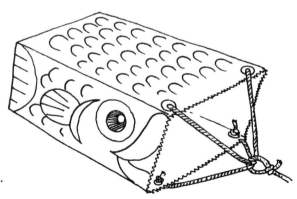

Ghost Tree

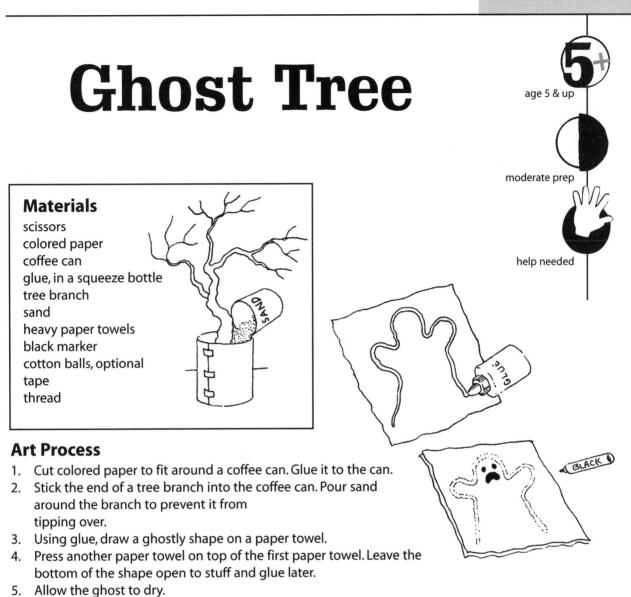

Materials
scissors
colored paper
coffee can
glue, in a squeeze bottle
tree branch
sand
heavy paper towels
black marker
cotton balls, optional
tape
thread

Art Process
1. Cut colored paper to fit around a coffee can. Glue it to the can.
2. Stick the end of a tree branch into the coffee can. Pour sand around the branch to prevent it from tipping over.
3. Using glue, draw a ghostly shape on a paper towel.
4. Press another paper towel on top of the first paper towel. Leave the bottom of the shape open to stuff and glue later.
5. Allow the ghost to dry.
6. Draw a face on the ghostly shape using a black marker.
7. Cut out the ghostly shape.
8. Stuff the shape with cotton balls using the opening at the bottom.
9. Glue the end closed.
10. Tape or stitch a piece of thread to the ghost's head and hang it from a tree branch.
11. Make more ghosts and hang them from the tree branches.

Variations
*   Make stuffed snowflakes, bears, hearts, or geometric shapes instead of ghosts. Experiment using different papers.
*   Trace your hand on double paper towels and make a ghost mitten or ghost puppet.

Hint
*   Sew paper towels together using a sewing machine instead of glue. Use a long stitch or a zigzag stitch.

Craft & Construction 47

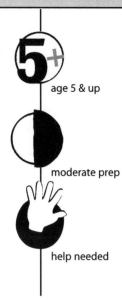

age 5 & up

moderate prep

help needed

Finger Puppets

Art Process

1. Cut two pieces of felt, about 3" x 2" (8 cm x 5 cm).
2. Place one piece of felt on top of the other piece and sew a zigzag stitch around them. Round the top and leave the bottom open to allow finger access.
3. Glue decorating materials to the puppet to create an animal, person, or character.
4. Draw features using markers.
5. Allow the puppet to dry.
6. Make up stories, plays, or dances and use the finger puppets as the main characters.

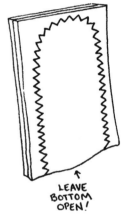

LEAVE BOTTOM OPEN!

Decorating Materials

buttons
craft eyes
fabric scraps
feathers
sequins

Variations

- Cut the fingers off an old glove and make each finger segment a puppet.
- Make puppets of characters from a favorite book and act out the story.
- Sing a song with the finger puppets.

Hint

- Some young artists may be able to sew the base together with supervision.

Stocking Mask

Materials

wire coat hanger
scissors
nylon stocking or panty hose
ribbons or rubber bands
glue or needle and thread
decorating materials (see list)

Art Process

1. Round out a wire coat hanger, moving the hook to the base, so that it resembles the shape of a hand mirror.
2. Cut the legs off a pair of stockings, then cut each stocking leg in half. Make two masks from each leg of a stocking.
3. To attach the stocking section with the foot, pull it over the hanger. Secure it with a ribbon or rubber band at the hooked end of the hanger.
4. To attach the thigh section of the stocking, secure both the top and the base of the stocking around the hanger.
5. Make a face on the stretched stocking by gluing or sewing decorating materials (see list) to the stocking.
6. Allow it to dry.
7. Hold up the stocking mask, hide your face behind it, and speak or act.

← IF THIGH SECTION IS USED...

Variation

- Cut out an oval shape from a piece of heavy cardboard. Cut out the middle of it and attach the stocking face. This material may not be as strong as a wire hanger, so cut the stocking into a single layer, then stretch and staple it to the cardboard.

Hints

- Very young children can be frightened of masks because they have not yet learned to separate fantasy from reality.
- Masks can make a shy child daring, a gentle child rough, a bold child quiet, or a rough child gentle.

Decorating Materials

beads
buttons
fabric scraps
old jewelry or earrings
paper clips
rug scraps
yarn

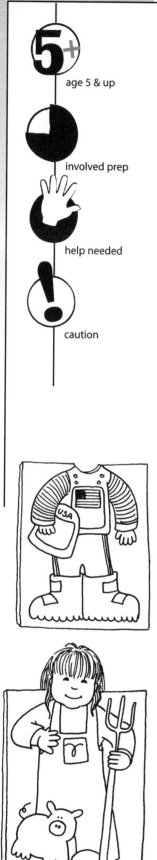

involved prep

help needed

caution

Peeky Panel

Art Process

1. Cut out a cardboard panel from a refrigerator or appliance box.
2. Trim the cardboard so it is chin-height of the artist.
3. Cut a half circle into the top edge of the cardboard.
4. Place the cardboard flat on the floor. Using chalk, sketch a comical or realistic human form. To change lines, simply rub off chalk and redraw them.
5. Cut the two circles into the cardboard for the hands or arms.
6. Place the cardboard flat on the floor again and paint the sketched body. Paint large areas first using a large, flat brush.
7. Allow the paint to dry. Then, use a small, fine brush to paint the smaller more refined areas.
8. Paint the background and additional details, such as an umbrella in the hand or a dog on a leash.
9. Allow the panel to dry again.
10. Stand behind the panel, insert your hands or arms through the two holes and rest your chin on the oval. Do this in front of a mirror or ask a friend take a picture.

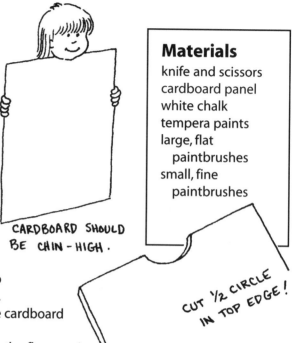

CARDBOARD SHOULD BE CHIN - HIGH.

CUT ½ CIRCLE IN TOP EDGE!

Materials

knife and scissors
cardboard panel
white chalk
tempera paints
large, flat
  paintbrushes
small, fine
  paintbrushes

Variation

• Cut out a face shape from a small piece of cardboard. Design this panel with hair, a hat, ears, jewelry, or other features. Use it as a mask.

Hint

• Young artists enjoy the comical possibilities of this art form. It will also help to expand their awareness of the human form.

Pressed Flower Frames

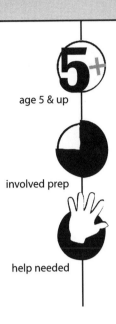
Materials

wooden curtain rings
heavy paper
pen
scissors
glue, in a squeeze bottle
dish
dried flowers, purchase or dry
    them (see instructions)
toothpicks

Art Process

1. Place a wooden curtain ring on a piece of heavy paper. Trace around the outside of the ring.
2. Cut out the circle, cutting it a little smaller than the drawn circle.
3. Squeeze some glue into a small dish.
4. Choose a dried flower and turn it upside down on the paper circle.
5. Dip the end of a toothpick into the glue and dot it lightly over the back of the flower. Carefully lift the flower and place it glue-side down onto the paper circle.
6. Repeat the process using as many flowers as desired.
7. Squeeze glue onto the back of the curtain ring. Lift the ring and stick it to the paper circle with the flowers. (Leave the screw eye of the ring at the top.)
8. Allow the project to dry.
9. The curtain ring makes a frame for the flower arrangement. If desired, use the screw eye as a wall hook.

Hints

- Pressed and dried flowers are delicate—handle them with care.
- Prepare ahead of time. Press flowers a month before starting this project.
- Young artists can do this project on their own, but they will likely need assistance gluing the ring to the paper.

GLUE ON BACK OF
FLOWER

CAREFULLY TURN OVER
FLOWER AND ATTACH TO
CENTER OF CIRCLE.

APPLY GLUE TO
CURTAIN RING.

Drying Flowers

fresh flowers
newspaper
heavy books or bricks

Place fresh flowers on a piece of newspaper, making sure the flowers do not touch each other. Put several layers of newspaper on top of the flowers. Lay heavy books or bricks on top of the newspaper and flowers. Allow the flowers to dry for about 4 weeks. (Thick flowers will take longer.)

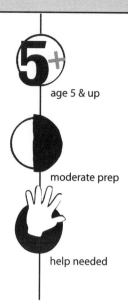

age 5 & up

moderate prep

help needed

Sea Scene

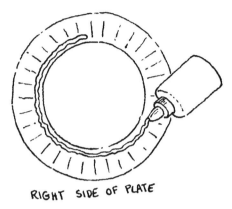

RIGHT SIDE OF PLATE

Art Process

1. Cut out the center of a paper plate, leaving the rim.
2. Turn the rim right side up and place glue along the inside edge.
3. Stretch a piece of clear plastic wrap over the opening in the plate and glue it down, creating a window effect.
4. Cut away the excess plastic when it has dried.
5. Color and cut out little fish, shells, and other sea creatures using the leftover piece of the plate.
6. Glue fish, yarn, sand, cellophane, or tissue onto the second plate.
7. Place the plate rim upside down on top of the full plate and staple around the outside.
8. Decorate the rim, if desired.

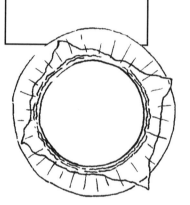

Variation

- Make other scenes such as family portraits, or display treasures or dried flowers.

Hints

- Artists will need help controlling the plastic wrap and the stapler.
- Use a glue gun to attach the second plate to the rim. Observe caution when using a glue gun.

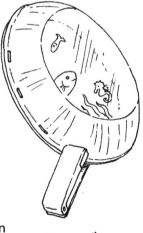

TURN "WINDOW" PLATE UPSIDE-DOWN, STAPLE TO DECORATED PLATE...

YOUR OWN PERSONAL AQUARIUM!!

Box Car

Materials

scissors
large cardboard
   box
tempera paint
paintbrushes
paper fasteners
paper plates
markers
aluminum foil
stapler or tape
heavy string

Art Process

1. Cut off the top flaps of a large cardboard box. Cut a hole in the bottom of the box. (Cut it large enough to fit over the artist's hips.)
2. Turn the box over so the hole is on top. Paint the box with any designs and allow the paint to dry.
3. Using scissors, poke four holes in the box to place the car wheels.
4. To make wheels, push paper fasteners through four paper plates and attach them to the holes in the box. Paint the wheels or decorate them with markers, if desired.
5. To make headlights, cover two paper plates with aluminum foil. Attach the headlights to the box using tape or paper fasteners. Tape over the pointed ends of the fasteners inside the box.
6. Poke a hole into each side of the top center of the box. Thread a piece of heavy string or cord through one of the holes. Tie it in a double knot so it cannot slip through the hole.
7. Step into the box car and pull it up to waist height. Pull the string around your back and over to the second hole. Tie another double knot.
8. The car will "hang" from your shoulders—it is ready to drive!

Hints

- This project involves a lot of work, but the amount of fun makes it worthwhile. Let the artists do as much as they can.
- Make sure the box car is completely dry before using it as a car. Keep in mind that the paint will still tend to smudge off onto damp or sweaty hands.

Craft & Construction   53

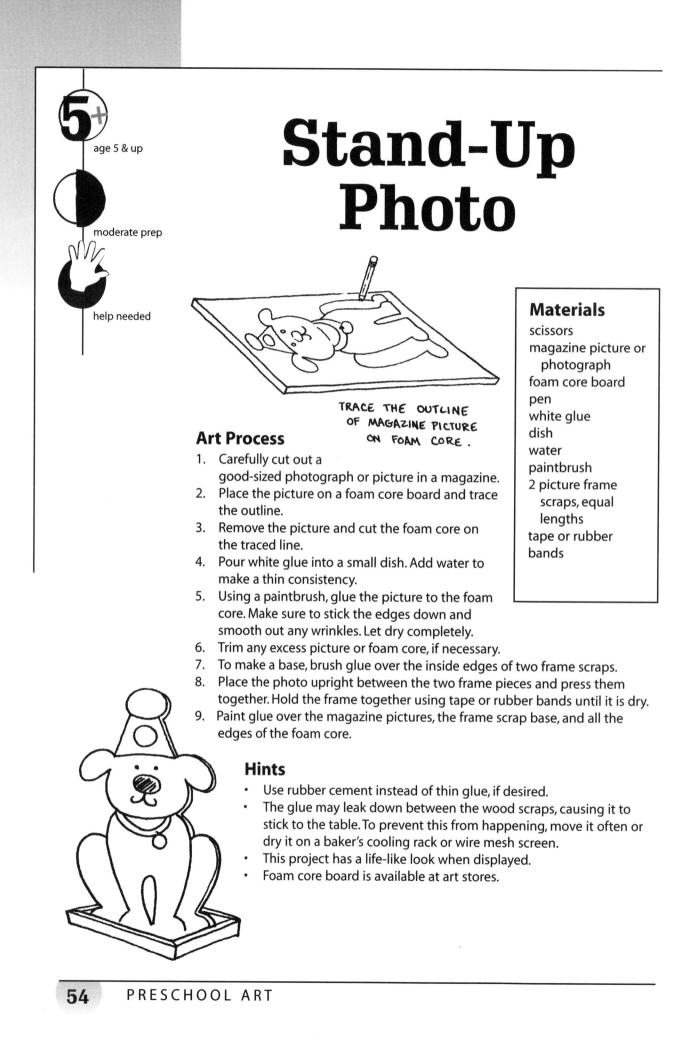

Stand-Up Photo

TRACE THE OUTLINE
OF MAGAZINE PICTURE
ON FOAM CORE.

Materials

scissors
magazine picture or
   photograph
foam core board
pen
white glue
dish
water
paintbrush
2 picture frame
   scraps, equal
   lengths
tape or rubber
bands

Art Process

1. Carefully cut out a good-sized photograph or picture in a magazine.
2. Place the picture on a foam core board and trace the outline.
3. Remove the picture and cut the foam core on the traced line.
4. Pour white glue into a small dish. Add water to make a thin consistency.
5. Using a paintbrush, glue the picture to the foam core. Make sure to stick the edges down and smooth out any wrinkles. Let dry completely.
6. Trim any excess picture or foam core, if necessary.
7. To make a base, brush glue over the inside edges of two frame scraps.
8. Place the photo upright between the two frame pieces and press them together. Hold the frame together using tape or rubber bands until it is dry.
9. Paint glue over the magazine pictures, the frame scrap base, and all the edges of the foam core.

Hints

- Use rubber cement instead of thin glue, if desired.
- The glue may leak down between the wood scraps, causing it to stick to the table. To prevent this from happening, move it often or dry it on a baker's cooling rack or wire mesh screen.
- This project has a life-like look when displayed.
- Foam core board is available at art stores.

Fabric Note Pad

Materials

scissors
heavy cardboard or thin wood
fabric scraps
white glue, in a squeeze bottle
dish
water
paintbrush
scraps of rickrack, lace, ribbon,
  and other notions
inexpensive, small note pad
small, dried flowers, optional
pencil
knife
paper fasteners
string
wall-hanging hook

Art Process
Making the Board—Part 1

1. Cut a piece of heavy cardboard or thin wood into a rectangular shape. Make sure it is at least twice as large as the note pad.
2. Cut fabric scraps into small squares and other shapes.
3. Pour glue into a small dish. Add water to make it a thin consistency.
4. Brush thinned glue over the fabric scraps and glue them all over the piece of cardboard. Use enough glue so it soaks through the fabric.
5. Glue rickrack, lace, or other notions around the edges of the cardboard to make a border.
6. Allow the project to dry overnight.

Adding the Note Pad—Part 2

1. Glue a small note pad to the center of the decorated cardboard.
2. If desired, glue dried flowers to the note pad board.
3. Using a pencil or knife, poke a hole into the cardboard.
4. Insert a paper fastener through the hole. Wrap one end of a piece of string around it.
5. Use a knife to cut a groove into the top end of a pencil and tie the other end of the string around the pencil groove (supervise closely). The pencil will hang on a string next to the note pad, ready to go to work.
6. Attach a wall-hanging hook to the back of the cardboard and hang it on the wall.

Hint

· Use a glue gun with supervision to attach decorations to the cardboard.

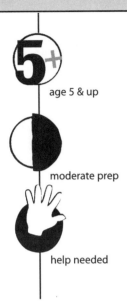

age 5 & up

moderate prep

help needed

Advent Boxes

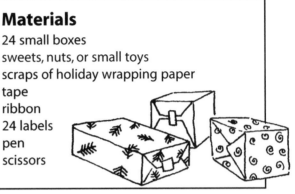

Materials
24 small boxes
sweets, nuts, or small toys
scraps of holiday wrapping paper
tape
ribbon
24 labels
pen
scissors

Art Process
1. Fill each of the 24 boxes with sweets, nuts, or small toys.
2. Wrap each box with scraps of wrapping paper and secure it with tape.
3. Tie each box with a ribbon. Curl the ends of the ribbons, if desired.
4. Place a label on each box and write the numbers 1-24 on each one.
5. Cut 24 long pieces of ribbon and tie one around each box.
6. Adjust the ribbons so that they hang at different lengths.
7. Gather all the ribbons into one hand, divide them into two bunches, and tie the two bunches together in a knot or bow.
8. Add a larger bow to the top of the Advent Box hanging, if desired.
9. Hang the Advent Boxes and open a box each day, starting on the first day of December. Open the 24th box on the day before Christmas.

Variation
• Put other items into the boxes, such as wishes for others, little drawings or pictures of holiday things, or greetings cut out of holiday cards.

Hints
• Jewelry boxes or matchboxes work well for this project.
• Most of this activity requires adult assistance. Artists will experience the most fun opening the boxes each day.
• Artists can wrap the boxes, but keep in mind that they will not do it the way adults would.

Boiled Paper Treasure Box

Materials

fabric dye, light color
hot water
pan
wrapping paper or shelf paper
stove
cardboard jewelry box
white glue
cup
paintbrush

Art Process—Boiled Paper

1. Dissolve fabric dye in hot water in a pan.
2. Crumple up wrapping paper and add it to the dye.
3. Boil the dye and paper on the stove for 5 minutes (supervise closely).
4. Rinse the paper in cold water.
5. Carefully squeeze the water from the paper.
6. Spread out the paper on a table or flat surface to dry. Dry paper will look like leather; use it in any papier-mâché project or to make the Treasure Box.

Art Process—Treasure Box

1. Turn a cardboard jewelry box and its lid upside down.
2. Pour white glue into a small dish. Dip a paintbrush into the glue and paint the box.
3. Cover the box with strips, torn pieces, or a large piece of the dry, boiled paper.
4. Place glue on the inside edges of the box.
5. Continue gluing boiled paper over the rim and inside the box. Cover the entire box and lid inside and out.
6. Allow the box to dry.
7. Use this leathery-looking box to store treasures.

Hints

- Make sure the box is thoroughly dry before placing the lid on it.
- Try not to put too much paper on the edge of the box or inside the lid or it may become too thick to fit back together.

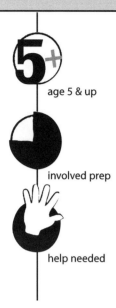

age 5 & up

involved prep

help needed

Papier-Mâché Bracelets

Art Process

1. Cut a cardboard strip about ½" to 2" (1.5 cm to 5 cm) wide. Then, cut it to fit around the widest part of your hand. (Leave enough room to allow for papier-mâché.)
2. Remove the strip, overlap the ends, and staple it together.
3. Pour wallpaper paste into a dish.
4. Tear newspaper into strips. Cut pieces of thin, white paper into strips about ½" to 2" (1.5 cm to 5 cm) long. Dip a piece of newspaper into the wallpaper paste and wrap it around the bracelet. Repeat this process, covering the bracelet with at least three layers of newspaper.
5. Cover the bracelet with strips of thin white paper to prevent the newsprint from showing through later. Add more paste, if necessary. Allow the bracelet to dry for several days.
6. Decorate the bracelet by painting or drawing on it. Or, cover it with liquid starch and pieces of colored tissue. Allow the bracelet to dry again.
7. If desired, paint the bracelet with a clear, glossy paint or polymer to add shine and protection.

Materials

scissors
cardboard
stapler
wallpaper paste
dish
newspaper
thin white paper
tempera paints and
  brushes
markers
colored tissue
paper
liquid starch
clear gloss enamel,
  optional

Hints

- Hang the bracelets over a cardboard tube, clothes hanger, or clothes-line to dry.
- Young artists may need help wrapping the papier-mâché around the bracelet strip.
- Papier-mâché is magical. It may be messy, but the fun will make it worthwhile.

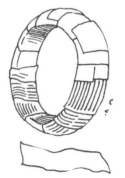

COVER NEWSPRINT WITH STRIPS OF WHITE PAPER

Index

Materials Index

liquid starch, 37, 58

M

magazine pictures or photographs, 54
margarine cup, 28
markers, 10, 11, 12, 14, 16, 21, 48, 52, 53, 58
    black, 47
    permanent, non-toxic, 13
masking tape, 9, 11, 15, 17, 20, 23, 26, 27, 28, 31, 36, 42
    wide, 39
matchboxes, 27, 56
matchsticks, 23
materials to weave, 44
materials to wrap, 26
materials with which to wrap, 26
matte board, 9, 10, 11, 28, 29
measuring cups, 22
metal cloth, 31
metal screen, 31
milk cartons, 20, 27
muffin tin, paper liners, 46

N

nail, 11, 24
    finishing, no head, 32
nails, large heads, 45
needle, plastic darning, 9, 15, 19, 30, 31, 34, 49
needle and thread, 34, 49
newspaper, 15, 21, 23, 39, 51, 58
note pad
    inexpensive, small, 55
notions, scrap, 55
nuts, 11, 22, 25
nuts, bolts, hardware items, 22
nuts, edible, 43, 56

O

outside items, 43
oven, 22
oven mitts, 22

P

paint, 16, 20, 21, 42
    tempera, 11, 20, 35, 36, 50, 53
paintbrushes, 10, 14, 20, 21, 25, 35, 36, 37, 38, 39, 42, 46, 53, 54, 55, 57, 58
    large, flat, 50
    old, 25
    small, fine, 50
paints, 16, 46
pan, 57
    baking, 23
pants, old with deep cuff or hem, 34
panty hose, 49
paper, 10, 16, 20, 24, 27, 30, 33, 36, 56
    art tissue, 52, 58
    bits, 43
    black, 24

butcher, 21
colored, 24, 39, 47
colored tissue, 38
construction, 36, 41
crepe paper, 17, 46
heavy, 10, 33, 51
hole punches, 19
muffin liners, 46
newspaper, newsprint, 15, 21, 23, 39, 51, 58
scrap, 19, 21
shelf liner, 57
stiff, 33
strips, 41
tissue, 37, 46
white, thin, 58
wrapping, 56, 57
paper clips, 25, 49
paper cutter, 42
paper fasteners, brads, 53, 55
paper plate basket holder, 30
paper plates, 16, 52, 53
paper punch, 9, 16, 41, 46
paper reinforcements, 46
paper scraps, 46
paper towel case box, 20
paper towels, heavy, 47
papier-mâché, 39, 58
paste
    wallpaper, 58
    wheat, 39
pencil, 15, 19, 22, 24, 40, 55
pens, 51, 54, 56
    fabric, 40
permanent markers, non-toxic, 13, 43
photographs, 54
pie plate, aluminum, 17
pieces of old toys, 11
pieces of toys, 10
pillow stuffing, 40
pin, 22, 24
pinking shears, 40
plastic bags, 27
plastic darning needles, 9, 15, 19, 30, 31, 34, 49
plastic eyes, 34
plastic needle, darning size, 19
plastic wrap, 20, 52
plastic, take-out food containers, 27
play clay, 43
pliable screen, 31
plywood, square, 45
poking tools, 15, 19, 24
powdered dye, 23

R

rack, baker's cooling, 54
raffia, 32
reinforcements, for paper, 46
reusable junk, 10
ribbon, 10, 11, 16, 26, 332, 44, 45, 46, 49, 55, 56
rickrack, 55
riding toys, variety, 17
rope, 45
rubber bands, 11, 25, 49, 54

rubber cement, 54
rubber gloves, 23
rug scraps, 49

S

sack, grocery, 46
safety glasses, 32, 38, 45
salt, 22
sand, 47, 52
scissors, 9, 14, 15, 18, 19, 20, 21, 24, 28, 29, 30, 31, 32, 33, 34, 36, 37, 40, 41, 42, 44, 46, 47, 48, 49, 50, 51, 52, 53, 54, 55, 56, 58
scissors point, 19
scooter, 17
scrapbook with blank pages, 12
scraps, 24
    butcher paper, 21
    colored tissue paper, 24
    fabric, 10, 29, 40, 48, 49, 55
    framing, 54
    holiday wrap, 56
    paper, 19, 21, 46
    picture frame, 54
    rug, 49
    sewing, 39, 55
    wood, 10, 11
    wood, flat, 32
    wood, thin, 55
screen, 31
    hamster cage variety, 31
    metal, 31
    pliable, 31
    wire mesh, 54
screen soffet, 31
screwdriver or chisel, 38
sequins, 48
sewing machine, 34, 35, 47, 48
sewing scraps, 34, 39, 55
sewing trims, 32, 55
sheet or linen, old, 35
shelf paper, 57
shoebox, 20
skewers, bamboo, 27, 24, 43
small cane basket, 30
small dish, 35, 38
small three-dimensional items, 25
small toys, 56
soap, liquid dish, 20
soffet screen, 31
spatula, 22
    wide, 23
spools, 10, 19
spoon, 35
spring-tension curtain rod (fits a doorway), 35
stapler, 21, 27, 40, 41, 52, 53, 58
stationery box, 20
sticks or branches, 20, 26
sticks, craft, 27
stick-on paper reinforcements, 27, 46
stiff paper, 33
stir sticks, wooden, 23
stockings, nylon (panty hose), 49

stove, 57
straws, 11, 19, 27
streamers, 16, 17, 26, 46
string, 16, 17, 18, 26, 27, 31, 43, 44, 45, 46, 55
    heavy string, 32, 53
strips of fabric, 32, 44
stuffing, for pillows, 40
Styrofoam
    blocks, 27
    grocery trays, 9, 10, 14, 15, 41
    pieces, 19
sweets, 56

T

tacky glue, 343, 35
tape, general, 12, 23, 24, 25, 26, 29, 39, 41, 47, 53, 54, 56
    masking tape, 9, 11, 15, 17, 20, 27, 28, 31, 36, 42
tempera paints, 10, 11, 35, 36, 37, 39, 50, 53, 58
thick tempera, 20
thin white paper, 58
thin wood, 55
thread, 47
three-dimensional items, 25
tiles, ceramic, white, 13
    from building contractors, scrap tile, 13
tin cans, 17
tissue paper, any, 38, 46
    colored tissue paper, 24, 37, 38, 52, 58
tongs, 23
toothpicks, 27, 43, 51
towel, damp, 39
toys, 22
    pieces of, 10
    small toys, 56
tray
    cardboard, 9
    Styrofoam grocery, 9, 10, 14, 15, 41
treats, 56
tricycle (trike), 17
tube, cardboard, 20, 58
twigs, 43

W

wagon, 17
wall-hanging hook, 55
wallpaper paste, 58
washers, 25
water, general, 18, 22, 38, 54, 55
    hot, 57
    puddle or pond, 27
    warm, 23
wax paper, 18
weaving materials, 32
weaving techniques, 32
weeds, 44
    dried, 22
wheat paste, 39
white ceramic tiles, 13
white chalk, 50
white glue, 14, 18, 20, 25, 27, 33, 38, 46, 48, 52, 54, 57

50 great ways to explore and create with playdough, tissue mâché, yeast dough, peanut butter dough, and more!

Clay and Dough

MaryAnn F. Kohl

Encourage children to experience the joy of exploration and discovery with this new series by award-winning author MaryAnn F. Kohl. Excerpted from the national best-seller **Preschool Art,** each book in the series emphasizes the process of art, not the product. **Preschool Art: Clay & Dough** gives you 50 great ways to create with playdough, tissue mâché, yeast dough, peanut butter dough, and more. Make art fun and accessible to children of all ages with these creative, easy-to-do activities!

ISBN 0-87659-250-7 / Gryphon House / 16928 / $7.95

50 great ways to explore and create with paper, feathers, buttons, and other easy-to-find materials!

Collage and Paper

MaryAnn F. Kohl

Encourage children to experience the joy of exploration and discovery with this new series by MaryAnn F. Kohl. Excerpted from the national best-sellers **Preschool Art** and **MathArts,** this book emphasizes the process of art, not the product. **Preschool Art: Collage and Paper** gives you 50 great ways to create with paper, feathers, buttons, and other easy-to-find materials. Make art fun and accessible to children of all ages with these creative, easy-to-do activities!

ISBN 0-87659-252-3 / Gryphon House / 15726 / $7.95

Available at your favorite bookstore, school supply store, or order from Gyphon House at 800.638.0928 or www.gryphonhouse.com.

50 great ways to explore and create using baking soda, shoe polish, vegetable dyes, and other surprising materials!

Painting
MaryAnn F. Kohl

Encourage children to experience the joy of exploration and discovery with this new series by award-winning author MaryAnn F. Kohl. Excerpted from the national best-seller **Preschool Art,** each book in the series emphasizes the process of art, not the product. **Preschool Art: Painting** brings you 50 great ways to paint using vegetable dyes, baking soda, cornstarch, shoe polish, and other surprising materials. Make art fun and accessible to children of all ages with these creative, easy-to-do activities!

ISBN 0-87659-224-8 / Gryphon House / 13596 / $7.95

50 great ways to explore and create with chalk, crayons, stencils, textures, and more!

Drawing

MaryAnn F. Kohl

Encourage children to experience the joy of exploration and discovery with this new series by award-winning author MaryAnn F. Kohl. Excerpted from the national best-seller **Preschool Art,** each book in this new series emphasizes the process of art, not the product. **Preschool Art: Drawing** gives you 50 great ways to create with chalk, crayons, stencils, textures, and more! Make art fun and accessible for children of all ages with these creative, easy-to-do activities.

ISBN 0-87659-223-X / Gryphon House / 19658 / $7.95

Available at your favorite bookstore, school supply store, or order from Gyphon House at 800.638.0928 or www.gryphonhouse.com.